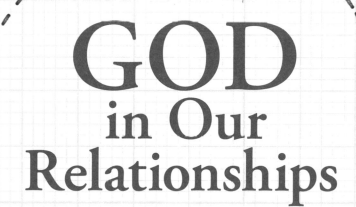

THE
GOSPEL
PROJECT.

GOD
in Our
Relationships
The Difference Maker

Rey De Armas

LifeWay Press®
Nashville, Tennessee

Item: 005688370
ISBN: 978-1-4300-3563-3
Dewey decimal classification number: 231.7
Subject heading: GOD \ TEN COMMANDMENTS \ SPIRITUAL LIFE

Eric Geiger
Vice President, Church Resources

Ed Stetzer
General Editor

Trevin Wax
Managing Editor

Faith Whatley
Director, Adult Ministry

Philip Nation
Director, Adult Ministry Publishing

Joel Polk
Content Editor

We believe that the Bible has God for its author; salvation for its end; and truth, without any mixture of error, for its matter and that all Scripture is totally true and trustworthy. To review LifeWay's doctrinal guideline, please visit *www.lifeway.com/doctrinalguideline.*

Unless otherwise noted, all Scripture quotations are taken from the Holman Christian Standard Bible®, copyright 1999, 2000, 2002, 2003, 2009 by Holman Bible Publishers. Used by permission.

For ordering or inquiries, visit *www.lifeway.com;* write LifeWay Small Groups; One LifeWay Plaza; Nashville, TN 37234-0152; or call toll free (800) 458-2772.

Printed in the United States of America.

Adult Ministry Publishing
LifeWay Church Resources
One LifeWay Plaza
Nashville, Tennessee 37234-0152

TABLE OF CONTENTS

ABOUT THE GOSPEL PROJECT AND WRITERS . . 4

HOW TO USE THIS STUDY 5

SESSION 1: 6
Our Relationship with Our Parents

SESSION 2: 18
Our Relationship with All of Life

SESSION 3: 30
Our Relationship within Marriage

SESSION 4: 42
Our Relationship with Possessions

SESSION 5: 54
Our Relationship with the Truth

SESSION 6: 66
Our Relationship with Our Desires

SMALL-GROUP TIPS AND VALUES 78

ABOUT THE GOSPEL PROJECT

Some people see the Bible as a collection of stories with morals for life application. But it's so much more. Sure, the Bible has some stories in it, but it's also full of poetry, history, codes of law and civilization, songs, prophecy, letters—even a love letter. When you tie it all together, something remarkable happens. A story is revealed. One story. The story of redemption through Jesus. This is *The Gospel Project*.

When we begin to see the Bible as the story of redemption through Jesus Christ, God's plan to rescue the world from sin and death, our perspective changes. We no longer look primarily for what the Bible says about us but instead see what it tells us about God and what He has done. After all, it's the gospel that saves us, and when we encounter Jesus in the pages of Scripture, the gospel works on us, transforming us into His image. *We become God's gospel project.*

ABOUT THE WRITERS

Rey De Armas serves as one of the campus pastors at Christ Fellowship in Miami, leading the Coral Gables campus. He is married to Lauren, and they have two daughters: Zoe and Lexi. During his free time, Rey enjoys dates with Lauren, playing with his daughters, and playing percussion.

Barry Cram adapted this material for use with small groups.

HOW TO USE THIS STUDY

Welcome to *The Gospel Project*, a gospel-centered small-group study that dives deep into the things of God, lifts up Jesus, focuses on the grand story of Scripture, and drives participants to be on mission. This small-group Bible study provides opportunities to study the Bible and to encounter the living Christ. *The Gospel Project* provides you with tools and resources to purposefully study God's Word and to grow in the faith and knowledge of God's Son. And what's more, you can do so in the company of others, encouraging and building up one another. Here are some things to remember that will help you maximize the usefulness of this resource:

GATHER A GROUP. We grow in the faith best in community with other believers, as we love, encourage, correct, and challenge one another. The life of a disciple of Christ was never meant to be lived alone, in isolation.

PRAY. Pray regularly for your group members.

PREPARE. This resource includes the Bible study content, three devotionals, and discussion questions for each session. Work through the session and devotionals in preparation for each group session. Take notes and record your own questions. Also consider the follow-up questions so you are ready to participate in and add to the discussion, bringing up your own notes and questions where appropriate.

RESOURCE YOURSELF. Make good use of the additional resources available on the Web at *www.gospelproject.com/additionalresources* and search for this specific title. Download a podcast. Read a blog post. Be intentional about learning from others in the faith.

GROUP TIME. Gather together with your group to discuss the session and devotional content. Work through the follow-up questions and your own questions. Discuss the material and the implications for the lives of believers and the mission to which we have been called.

OVERFLOW. Remember …*The Gospel Project* is not just a Bible study. *We* are the project. The gospel is working on us. Don't let your preparation time be simply about the content. Let the truths of God's Word soak in as you study. Let God work on your heart first, and then pray that He will change the hearts of the other people in your group.

THE GOSPEL PROJECT

Session 1

Our Relationship with Our Parents

While on the cross, [Jesus] commits his mother to the disciple, teaching us to show every care for our parents even to our last breath.[1]

JOHN CHRYSOSTOM (CIRCA 347–407)

INDIVIDUAL STUDY

The Bible speaks to every aspect of life—including the family. God has something to say about our relationship with our parents. After all, He's the One who chose who our parents would be. And no matter our experience with our mother and father, God's Word speaks to us giving instruction on our attitude toward them.

Watch movies and television long enough, and you'll notice the different depictions of parents. Some stories reflect writers' idealistic views of parenthood. Other stories are a projection of the writer's own difficult relationships with his or her parents. Think of the current television shows that claim to be about the family. Each show has a different perspective on the roles of father and mother. If our media choices shape us more than God's Word, we're more likely to have a skewed vision of our parents. And how we view our parents will often determine how we treat them.

> **What image comes to mind when you think of parenthood? Does it line up with a view that honors or tears down?**

In the Fifth Commandment, God promises life to those who honor their father and mother. We obey this Commandment by respecting the authority God has given our parents and by caring for them in their old age. Honoring our parents is also a way we reflect Jesus Christ. He perfectly loved and honored His mother and father.

In this session, we'll see that our parents are put in place by God to guide us and love us. Our respect for our parents demonstrates our love for them, in the same way that our reverence for our Heavenly Father demonstrates our love for Him. It's important that we recognize that God's Word is clear as to how we should treat our parents—in a way that honors both them and the Lord.

Over the next week, engage the daily study material. These three sessions center on how to find God in our relationships with our parents. Interact with the Scriptures, and be ready to interact with your small group.

1 Parental Authority is God Given

Honor your father and mother, as the LORD your God has
commanded you, so that you may live long and so that you may
prosper in the land the LORD your God is giving you.
DEUTERONOMY 5:16

The Fifth Commandment is different from the other nine for at least two reasons—it
comes with both a tag and a promise. First, let's look at the tag: "as the LORD your God
has commanded you." The other commands don't refocus attention on God as the Source
of their authority. All Ten Commandments are from God, but here extra care is given to
reinforce the truth that God is the One commanding us to obey our parents.

Next, let's look at the promise: "so that you may live long and so that you may prosper in the
land the LORD your God is giving you." Long life and prosperity come from honoring our
parents. God provides an incentive to obey this command. In the Old Testament the punishment for dishonoring your parents was serious. In some cases dishonorable children were
put to death for rebelling against their parents (see Deut. 21:18-21). Just as disobedience
led to death in the garden of Eden, disobedience to one's parents would lead to death in the
promised land. On the other hand, obedience would prolong life and freedom.

**What are some of the blessings children receive when they honor and
obey their parents?**

What are the blessings we receive as adults who honor our parents?

This Commandment reveals a foundational way we can honor God in our relationships.
We do this by placing His design for family over our sinful nature. In other words, we honor
God by honoring our parents. Because God is the One who put this command in place, we
can honor and obey God through our obedience to our parents. As we get older and more
independent, we may find it hard to believe this command still applies to us. But honoring
our parents is a lifelong endeavor that God wants us to pursue with obedience.

We should remember that obedience with a poor attitude isn't honor. There is such a thing as
disrespectful obedience, and it's not what God desires. God doesn't just want our actions to

be right while our hearts are not. If obedience were enough, then God would have said "obey" your parents. But He didn't. This Commandment implies a respectful posture toward those who have authority over us.

Why are we prone to disrespect authority as children and teenagers?

What are some examples of a respectful posture toward authority?

Many Christians are discouraged by the idea of keeping this Commandment. Why? It's because their parents have led them to adopt a distorted view of God. This command can be especially difficult for those who grew up without fathers or mothers who provided, protected, and cared for them. Still, it's possible to honor our parents even when they make mistakes. The Bible doesn't tell us to honor our parents because they are always right, it tells us to honor them because God has commanded it.

Scripture isn't silent toward those who suffer at the hands of bad parents. God knows our pain, and He desires to fill the void left by an absent or abusive parent. Psalm 27:10 says, "Even if my father and mother abandon me, the LORD cares for me." Good parents reflect God by comparison. Bad parents reflect God by contrast. Either way, God desires to show us all a divine love that's far greater than that of any parent. And He has demonstrated His love through the giving of His Son.

How does your relationship with your parents impact how you view God?

How can we show respect to parents who do not deserve respect?

How have the roles of father and mother changed in pop culture over the years? Do you see the trajectory as positive or negative? Why?

2 Bring Joy to Those Who Gave You Life

So we see that this Fifth Commandment to honor our father and mother doesn't lose its relevance when we leave home. We're to honor our parents as long as they live. This isn't something we grow out of. Even when we begin families of our own, it's important that we honor our parents. The Bible shows us how in Proverbs 23:

> ²² Listen to your father who gave you life,
>   and don't despise your mother when she is old.
> ²³ Buy—do not sell—truth, wisdom, instruction, and understanding.
>   ²⁴ The father of a righteous son will rejoice greatly,
>   and one who fathers a wise son will delight in him.
>   ²⁵ Let your father and mother have joy,
>   and let her who gave birth to you rejoice.
>   **PROVERBS 23:22-25**

Previous generations provide wisdom that helps guide our future. Throughout the Book of Proverbs, readers are encouraged to listen to the wisdom of their parents. The writer encourages his son to apply wisdom to his life. In heeding the wisdom and instruction we receive from previous generations, we can avoid troublesome mistakes.

What practical ways can we show respect to our parents in their old age?

Later in life, we honor God by caring for our parents. Paul said: "But if anyone does not provide for his own, that is his own household, he has denied the faith and is worse than an unbeliever" (1 Tim. 5:8). God is serious about caring for family. This isn't just a command; it's a warning to examine our hearts to see if we are truly believers. We are to honor our parents by caring for those who once cared for us.

As parents, we must make sure we are reflecting God in how we treat our children. We answer to God for how we lead our families. Our kids are gifts from God, and He has given us the responsibility to bring them up in the Lord. In Ephesians 6:4, following the restatement of the command to honor our fathers and mothers, the apostle Paul wrote that fathers should not stir up anger in their children but instead bring them up in the training of the Lord. Here are some verses that speak of a parent's responsibility to treat children in a manner similar to how God has treated us:

Teach them the way of the Lord.

> [4] Listen, Israel: The LORD our God, the LORD is One. [5] Love the LORD your
> God with all your heart, with all your soul, and with all your strength. [6] These
> words that I am giving you today are to be in your heart. [7] Repeat them
> to your children. Talk about them when you sit in your house and when
> you walk along the road, when you lie down and when you get up.
> DEUTERONOMY 6:4-7

Discipline them in love.

> [12] For the LORD disciplines the one He loves, just as a father, the son he delights
> in. [13] Happy is a man who finds wisdom and who acquires understanding.
> PROVERBS 3:12-13

Provide for them.

> [9] What man among you, if his son asks him for bread, will give him a
> stone? [10] Or if he asks for a fish, will give him a snake? [11] If you then, who
> are evil, know how to give good gifts to your children, how much more
> will your Father in heaven give good things to those who ask Him.
> MATTHEW 7:9-11

Jesus compared God's love for us to the way we provide good gifts to our children. He spoke of prayer by appealing to a parental principle that is universally recognized—even imperfect parents give good gifts to their children. From this we recognize that parents should never intentionally harm their children but instead provide for them in a way that lovingly reflects the Father's heart.

How does the gospel impact the way we care for our parents? How does the gospel impact the way we parent our children?

How does our experience of forgiveness free us from living in regret and empower us to fulfill our responsibilities as parents and/or children?

3 Honor Parents as Christ Honored His

Caring for our parents reflects the very heart of Jesus. We can see the love Jesus had for His mother, especially at the cross:

> 25 Standing by the cross of Jesus were His mother, His mother's sister, Mary the wife of Clopas, and Mary Magdalene. 26 When Jesus saw His mother and the disciple He loved standing there, He said to His mother, "Woman, here is your son." 27 Then He said to the disciple, "Here is your mother." And from that hour the disciple took her into his home.
>
> JOHN 19:25-27

Imagine the difficulty of living through this moment. Put yourself in the scene as you watch the child you raised suffer and die a horrifying death. Mary mourned the loss of her child, but she was not alone. In this moment of physical torment, Jesus took time to demonstrate love to His mother. He acknowledged her presence and commissioned one of His disciples to care for her.

This powerful scene depicts the close relationship Jesus had with both Mary and the disciple He loved (most likely, John). If you were going to ask someone to take care of your mother, you would probably turn to a close friend. There would need to be a solid, trusting relationship between the one making the command to care and the caretaker.

We reflect the Savior when we put the needs of others above our own. In this moment, Jesus could have been focused on His own situation as He endured the agony of the cross. But even here we see His self-giving love. He placed the needs of His mother above His own. In this event He demonstrated what honoring one's parents looks like. Even in death, Jesus was obedient to God's commands.

What do we learn from Christ's love for His parents?

Why is it important to see in this story that Jesus is an example of love and also the Savior who forgives our failure to love?

In Jesus, we receive the love and acceptance we have craved from our parents. Whether your parents were present or absent, you understand the deep human longing we all have for affection. Only the love that Jesus provides is great enough to fill our need.

Too many times we see God the Father as a demanding tyrant who is never satisfied with our obedience. Always disappointed, He hovers over us with a rod of punishment. The gospel doesn't change our view of God; it reinforces what has always been true about God! Because of Jesus, we know that God loves us as His children. The Father sees us through His Son.

We often strive for acceptance and affection from our earthly parents. Thankfully, the love of Christ provides fulfillment that is greater and lasts longer than even the love our parents can provide. Not only that, the sacrifice of Christ covers our own failures as parents.

What are some of your regrets in how you have treated your parents?

What about your children? How does the gospel apply to those regrets?

How does a Christian understanding of authority differ from that of the world?

GROUP STUDY

Warm Up

Honor your father and mother.
DEUTERONOMY 5:16

Honor your father and mother, which is the first commandment with a promise.
EPHESIANS 6:2

The root word for *honor* in this passage is the Hebrew word *kabad*—which is the same word used for *glory* in the Old Testament. The idea here is to give something weight or make it heavy. This means children should hold their parents in high esteem. Also make note the verb is an imperative—which emphasizes the force of the command. It indicates there is no exception to the rule. The command doesn't depend on how the parents respond to the child. We are to honor our parents regardless if they have earned it or deserve it. We honor our parents out of respect, honor, and obedience to God.

> Who do you know in your life (friends or family) that has personified this command? In what ways did they "give weight" to their parents and honor them?

> What does God's promise look like to you?

As parents age, it is important that we remember to show them the honor they deserve. It can be easy to forget about our parents as we grow. Time becomes scarce. The distractions of life can keep us from showing love and honor toward those who provided for us in childhood. God does not promise our parents will be around forever. But He does give a promise to those who honor their parents for as long as they live.

Discussion

When you stop and think about it, the Fifth Commandment is God's way of extending this privilege of living with Him through us toward our parents. Through Christ, we have received the spirit of adoption as sons, and now have the right to address God as Father (see Rom. 8:15). As sons and daughters of God, we have a new kind of relationship with the Father—not as enemies but as family (see Rom. 5:10). So as we respond to God in obedience to the Fifth Commandment, we also reflect the kind of relationship we have with God to our parents. And we are all drawn closer to God.

Use this time to share what God has revealed as you connect the dots and pursue the gospel. The questions below are from your daily reading assignments. They will guide your small-group discussion.

1. How does your relationship with your parents impact how you view God? How can we show respect to parents who do not deserve respect?

2. How have the roles of father and mother changed in pop culture over the years? Do you see the trajectory as positive or negative?

3. What are some practical ways we can show respect to our parents in their old age? What do we communicate about ourselves if we are indifferent to our parents?

4. How does the gospel impact the way we care for our parents? How does the gospel impact the way we parent our children?

5. Do you think our culture as a whole honors and respects the elderly? Why or why not?

6. How does our experience of forgiveness free us from living in regret and empower us to fulfill our responsibilities as parents and/or children?

7. What do we learn from Christ's love for His parents? Why is it important to see in this story that Jesus is an example of love and also the Savior who forgives our failure to love?

Conclusion

How does honoring our parents impact our mission? In a day and age when children and teenagers are expected to rebel, we put forth a vision of adolescence that emphasizes obedience and honor. In a culture that despises the elderly, we put forth a vision of old age that emphasizes wisdom and respect. Our mission is enhanced by how we treat those in authority over us. In honoring our parents, we demonstrate to a watching world the power of the gospel of Jesus Christ.

Spend some time praying this for you and for your group:

> "God, I need You to help me in this. Give me the ability to show the respect and honor You want me to give to my parents. Let my relationship with my parents be a reflection of the gospel to others. Help me to forgive where there needs to be forgiveness. Amen."

1. St. John Chrysostom, as found in *A Select Library of the Nicene and Post-Nicene Fathers of the Christian Church*, ed. by Philip Schaff (New York: The Christian Literature Company, 1890), 318.

2. Sir Arthur Conan Doyle, *The Adventures and Memoirs of Sherlock Holmes* (New York: The Modern Library, 1920), 327-28

I have frequently gained my first real insight into the character of parents by studying their children.[2]

SIR ARTHUR CONAN DOYLE

NOTES

_____

_____

_____

_____

_____

_____

_____

_____

_____

_____

_____

_____

_____

THE
GOSPEL PROJECT

Session 2

Our Relationship with All of Life

Whoever hates is a murderer. You may not have prepared
any poison or committed a crime. You have only hated,
and in doing so, you have killed yourself first of all.[1]

AUGUSTINE (354-430)

INDIVIDUAL STUDY

It's almost impossible to watch the news without seeing stories of the devaluing of human life across the world. Murders happen frequently for reasons that involve the heart—desire for power, for passion, or for possessions. No matter the case, it's clear from history and our own experience that we need God to reiterate something we already instinctively know to be true—human life is valuable, and people should not murder.

In 2011, it was reported by *The New York Times* that two different US government agencies adjusted their numerical dollar amount for the value of a human life. The Environmental Protection Agency set the value of a life at $9.1 million in 2010 in order to propose higher air pollution restrictions. That same year, the Food and Drug Administration chose to value life at $7.9 million in order to propose that warning labels on cigarette packages should feature pictures of cancer victims.[2]

> **What factors do you consider when determining the value of human life? Do you consider some lives more or less valuable than others? Why or why not?**

Instead of a dollar amount, what if human lives were valued in minutes? The Sci-Fi movie *In Time* (2011) gives a glimpse into a bleak future where at the age of 25, a person's biological clock begins counting down. Time becomes a form of currency that people trade for goods and services. In a very literal sense, "time is money!" In this story, the human body never displays any form of aging, but when a person's individual clock reaches zero, they die. The film is filled with suspense as the characters in the movie battle over time.

Although we do not treat time as currency, we do speak of it as such. Time is *spent*, *stolen*, *invested*, and *saved*. And this is fitting because your life—the sum total of your time on earth—is valuable to God. Because all human life is valuable, taking someone's life in the wrong fashion has dire consequences in Scripture.

Throughout the week engage these daily study sections on your own. Each of them answers different questions about the Sixth Commandment. There are three daily readings to prepare you before the group meets for this session. Interact with the Scriptures, and be ready to interact with your small group.

What is Murder?

In Deuteronomy 5, Moses recounted the giving of the Ten Commandments to the people of Israel. He noted the serious nature of the event by reminding the people how they had been afraid of God's fiery presence on the mountain—to the point they could not go up on the mountain to speak with the Lord themselves. So Moses acted as the mediator. He presented the Lord's commands in order to help the nation of Israel understand the laws that God established to govern them. But the Lord Himself spoke from the fire when He gave the Ten Commandments to the people (5:22), including this Commandment:

> Do not murder.
> **DEUTERONOMY 5:17**

This Commandment is clear and concise. It leaves little room for ambiguity. Yet there are qualifications that Scripture makes elsewhere. In this case, we must examine the difference between murder and killing. Although both end with the demise of a human being, killing is governed by God's laws and the principles laid out in His Word. Murder, however, is condemned as a sin because of the motive that lies behind it. It disregards the inherent value of human life as created by God.

> How would you describe the difference between murder and killing?
> What biblical examples help illustrate the differences?

In our context, it seems almost unnecessary that God would need to emphasize the importance of life through a Commandment. But when you examine the other nine Commandments, you begin to see that Israel, and humanity in general, needed God to teach them what it meant to be human.

God grounded this Commandment in the unique nature of His creation of humankind. Genesis 9:6 says, "Whoever sheds man's blood, his blood will be shed by man, for God made man in His image." This command traces our value for human life back to the creation account. Prior to breathing life into Adam, God revealed the value of human life. "Let Us make man in Our image, according to our likeness" (1:26). And as bearers of the image of God, human beings are unique in creation. Man is created lower than God, and yet he is given dominion over the earth. We were uniquely designed to tend to the rest of God's creation. This is why we were made. We are to honor and reflect God's image by valuing the life that He has given.

So are there exceptions? We must account for situations in which killing doesn't fall under the category of murder—self-defense, capital punishment, and just war. We'll take a brief look at these through the lens of Scripture. Notice that anger is absent in each circumstance.

Self-Defense. We see in Scripture that a person is allowed to defend him or herself from an attacker (see Neh. 4:11-14). Exodus 22:2-3 reads, "If a thief is caught in the act of breaking in, and he is beaten to death, no one is guilty of bloodshed. But if this happens after sunrise, there is guilt of bloodshed." So even after the Ten Commandments are given in Exodus 20, we can see that God permits the taking of a life if one's own life is in potential danger.

Capital Punishment. Even before the law was given to Israel, God established the notion of capital punishment. Genesis 9:6 points out that if a man kills another man, his life should also be taken. This punishment speaks to the severity of the crime. The taking of a life warrants a punishment in kind—a death for a death. The command isn't given for vengeance but for justice, and the role of justice is carried out by one specific office—governments with just laws. Paul makes the obvious observation in Romans 13:4 that "government is God's servant for your good. But if you do wrong, be afraid, because it does not carry the sword for no reason. For government is God's servant, an avenger that brings wrath on the one who does wrong." The "sword" belongs to the governing authorities to wield and to deliver justice to those who commit evil.

Just War. In Scripture, God at times commanded battles between nations. Such battles and wars were God's hand of justice against the wicked. Examples of God sanctioning war can be found throughout the historical books of the Old Testament. Although men and women are killed in battle, there must be a difference between the act of murder and a death in battle. Christ doesn't ask that His followers stand and fight for physical territory or possessions. However, there is an understanding that kingdoms of the world have servants who go out and fight, and Christians aren't necessarily exempt from participating in military actions.

> What does Jesus teach concerning the issue of self-defense? How can we defend ourselves and love our enemies at the same time?

> How would you define a just war? If a war were determined to be unjust, how should Christians respond?

2 What Motivation is Behind Murder?

If killing in the context of war, capital punishment, or self-defense is permissible in the Old Testament, what, then, distinguishes murder? Murder goes deeper than the death of a human being by the hand of another human being. Murder is the crime of unlawfully killing a person—especially with malice or forethought. Murder, therefore, is distinguished from killing by the issue of motive.

Jesus identified that motive in Matthew 5:21-22:

> 21 "You have heard that it was said to our ancestors, Do not murder,
> and whoever murders will be subject to judgment. 22 But I tell you,
> everyone who is angry with his brother will be subject to judgment. And
> whoever says to his brother, 'Fool!' will be subject to the Sanhedrin.
> But whoever says, 'You moron!' will be subject to hellfire.

Christ goes to the root of the behavior and sees the anger behind the action. The act of murder is still subject to the punishment we see in Genesis 9:6, yet Christ takes an extra step by declaring that the person who feels anger toward his brother will also be subject to judgment. So murder is not just about the action of killing a human being but the motive that lies behind the action as well.

It's a dangerous path that leads one down to murder. When emotion supersedes the value of life, a murder can take place. When a murder takes place, the image of God in humanity is denied through action. And Satan is delighted by this. Why? It's because God's handiwork is destroyed through sin. In John 8:44, Jesus called Satan a murderer from the beginning.

Why does Christ place emphasis on our motives?

How has the gospel changed the motives behind your actions?

The anger that could lead to murder is sinful. The same sinful anger can lead to other actions as well. For this reason, Jesus recognized the power of words in Matthew 5:22 by warning His disciples of their effects. We need to take into account how our words affect others, but we also need to understand that we're held accountable for our words. Christ said that we will be accountable and subject to judgment for harshly insulting a brother or sister.

James 3:9-10 says, "We praise our Lord and Father with [the tongue], and we curse men who are made in God's likeness with it. Praising and cursing come out of the same mouth. My brothers, these things should not be this way." Yes, God cares about the very words we use to describe those whom He has created. Words spoken in hatred are prohibited because it is an attack on the image of God in humanity.

Words are important, though often taken for granted. Our words can breathe life into an individual, or they can kill confidence. Proverbs 18:21 reminds us, "Life and death are in the power of the tongue, and those who love it will eat its fruit." Our words are powerful. Use them wisely.

We don't have the "power to create" with words like those spoke by God. But our words do contain power. Describe how you have used your words in a powerful way.

When have you used words in an angry way? What were the effects?

3 What is the Solution to a Hateful Heart?

We know that hate is the motive behind murder. First John 3:10-15 tells us how a hateful heart can lead to hurtful actions. It also tells us that the gospel of Jesus Christ can change the motives of the heart.

> [10] This is how God's children—and the Devil's children—are made evident. Whoever does not do what is right is not of God, especially the one who does not love his brother. [11] For this is the message you have heard from the beginning: We should love one another, [12] unlike Cain, who was of the evil one and murdered his brother. And why did he murder him? Because his works were evil, and his brother's were righteous. [13] Do not be surprised, brothers, if the world hates you. [14] We know that we have passed from death to life because we love our brothers. The one who does not love remains in death. [15] Everyone who hates his brother is a murderer, and you know that no murderer has eternal life residing in him.
>
> **1 JOHN 3:10-15**

Cain's works were evil. They came from an evil heart motivated by anger. We are all capable of such anger. Our sinfulness can drive us to the brink of human behavior, causing us to commit the most heinous of crimes. Just as Cain killed his brother, we are all capable of murder.

> John cites Cain as an illustration of the absence of love, which marks the child of the devil. The apostle's choice of Cain ... demonstrates the antithetical natures of the children of God and the children of 'the evil one.' Cain is identified as being 'of the evil one' ... Cain belonged to the evil one, to the devil, a thought that apparently is derived from Genesis 4:7, where God warns Cain that 'sin is crouching at your door.' The adjective ['evil'] indicates the active exercise of evil in one's behavior. Cain demonstrated the defining actions of his spiritual father.[3]
>
> **DANIEL L. AKIN**

Jesus was placed on a cross by His enemies. Though they intended evil, God brought about the ultimate good. We see the love of Christ in His sacrifice on the cross. He willingly laid down His life, faced His accusers as He was mocked and scorned, and endured death, only to be raised again on the third day.

The children of God are motivated and known by their love, rather than anger. This love can only stem from the gospel. The saving work of Christ is the only thing that can take an evil heart and cause it to be motivated by love. First John 3:16 says, "This is how we have come to know love: He laid down His life for us. We should also lay down our lives for our brothers." It's through this that we resemble Christ and not Cain. Christ laid down His life for us and gave life. As Christians, we don't take life from others, either by our actions or our words; we lay down our lives for our brothers and sisters as Christ did.

How should our motivation contrast that of the world? How does the attitude of Christ contrast with the attitude of Cain?

How can we love others when we are tempted to become angry?

What is the church's responsibility in a community to address the issue of murder?

How might we communicate the love of Christ to those guilty of murder?

GROUP STUDY

Warm Up

A murder in a neighborhood will affect the entire community, not just the individual families involved. We believe this about the murders of celebrities or political figures—Nicole Brown Simpson or President John F. Kennedy. But it is no less true concerning everyone else. Nations are shaken to their core whenever a murder takes place at a school. At one time, Sandy Hook Elementary and Columbine High School were just quiet schools in quiet neighborhoods. Now they represent events that darken the United States' history, expose our fallen state, and fuel our demand for justice.

How do we process the sin of murder on a national conversation?

In what ways do we look for answers when we witness such "senseless violence"?

Think about the different ways we can turn the conversation toward God. Discuss how God can show up in these kinds of conversations.

We are all connected. It wasn't just those who died who were affected. Moms and dads lost their children. Communities grieved over the loss of friends. Whenever such atrocities take place, we are brought into a state of disarray over the human condition. We instinctively react because we inherently value all human life. And it continually reminds us all that we need the saving grace of Jesus Christ through the power of the gospel.

Discussion

Our world is full of people who do not know that they are made in the image of God and valuable to Him. They do not fully recognize the eternal consequences of the anger in their hearts. They may not even fully see how their hatred extends to God Himself. Yet as Jesus loved us enough to die for us while we were still His enemies, we ought to love these people in the name of Jesus that they too may be freed from hatred to love God and others.

During this time you will have an opportunity to discuss what God revealed to you during the week. Listed below are some of the questions from your daily reading assignments. They will guide your small-group discussion.

1. How would you describe the difference between murder and killing? What biblical examples help illustrate the differences?

2. What does Jesus teach concerning the issue of self-defense? How can we defend ourselves and love our enemies at the same time?

3. Why does Christ place emphasis on our motives? How has the gospel changed the motives behind your actions?

4. We do not have the "power to create" with words like those spoke by God. But our words do contain power. Describe how you have used your words in a powerful way.

5. When have you used words in an angry way? What were the effects?

6. How should our motivation contrast that of the world? How does the attitude of Christ contrast with the attitude of Cain? How can we love others when we are tempted to become angry?

7. What is the church's responsibility in a community to address the issue of murder? How might we communicate the love of Christ to those guilty of murder?

Conclusion

Because we are made in the image of God, murder is a sin. We have studied the Sixth Commandment from God and understand the value of human life. Jesus showed how the sin of murder begins with anger in the human heart. And through the gospel, love overcomes hate. We are set free to love our brothers and sisters in the way God originally intended.

Love is the great divide between the children of God and the children of the devil. Those who have love are children of God, and those who do not are children of the devil. Have anything else you like, but if you lack this one thing, then all the rest is of no use to you whatsoever. On the other hand, you may lack almost anything else, but if you have this one thing, you have fulfilled the law.[4]

BEDE (CIRCA 673-735)

Spend some time praying this for you and for your group:

"God, You know my motives. Help me to value all of life. Reveal to me any unconfessed bitterness, hatred, or anger in my heart. Give me words to build up, not tear down. In all of this, help me love my enemies as You have loved me. Amen."

1. Augustine, Sermons 49.7, *Works of St. Augustine: A Translation for the Twenty-First Century*, ed. J. E. Rotelle (Hyde Park, NY: New City Press, 1995), 3/2:338, quoted in *James, 1–2 Peter, 1–3 John, Jude,* ed. Gerald Bray, vol. XI in *Ancient Christian Commentary on Scripture: New Testament* (Downers Grove: InterVarsity Press 2000), 203.
2. Benyamin Appelbaum, "As U.S. Agencies Put More Value on a Life, Businesses Fret," *The New York Times*, February 16, 2011. Online. *http://www.nytimes.com/2011/02/17/business/economy/17regulation.html?pagewanted=all&_r=0*
3. Daniel Akin, *1, 2, 3 John: An Exegetical and Theological Exposition of Holy Scripture* (Nashville: B&H, 2001), 154-156.
4. Bede, as quoted in *Ancient Christian Commentary on Scripture, New Testament*, vol. XI, ed. Gerald Bray and Thomas C. Oden (Downers Grove: InterVarsity Press, 2000), 201.
5. Doug McIntosh, *Deuteronomy, vol. 3* in *Holman Old Testament Commentary* (Nashville: B&H, 2002), 72.

Murder is, among other things, the usurping of a prerogative that is reserved for God alone. He gives life and takes it. For a person to murder another is to set himself up as a rival to God himself.[5]

DOUG MCINTOSH

NOTES

_____

_____

_____

_____

_____

_____

_____

_____

_____

_____

_____

_____

_____

THE GOSPEL PROJECT

Session 3

Our Relationship within Marriage

As believers, through Christ we have been made worthy to be a place that God is pleased to dwell. In light of this, we must be driven to live a life reflecting who is inside of us.[1]

ERIC MASON

INDIVIDUAL STUDY

Not long ago, a commercial came out for Pepsi Max® that depicted two truck drivers eating at the same diner. One truck driver represented Pepsi Max and the other represented Coca Cola Zero®. The Pepsi guy strikes up a conversation with the Coke guy while the song "Why Can't We Be Friends?" plays from the jukebox. Next, the Pepsi driver offers a Pepsi Max to his newfound friend (who happens to be wearing a Coca Cola hat and uniform). Thinking this is a sign of true friendship, the Coke driver takes a large swig of the soda. But the Pepsi driver records the other driver with his phone, posts the video to YouTube®, and then tells the guy what he did. The commercial ends with the two men launching out of the diner window in a brawl.

The reason the Pepsi Max commercial is so effective is because we see the Coca Cola driver "cheating" on his company. In reality, of course, he was just drinking another soda. He wasn't married to the product. Even though he wouldn't be legally prohibited from drinking Pepsi, there was irony in his actions. We expect fidelity from him, even without an oath or commitment!

> In society, fidelity is often an unspoken expectation. How does our culture define fidelity and betrayal?

> How do you measure your faithfulness to those important to you— friends, family, parents, co-workers, boss?

Scripture has much to say about fidelity, oaths, and commitment. But Scripture's focus is on more important things than brand loyalty for certain teams or companies or products. First, God desires for us to be faithful to Him, to put no other gods before Him, and live in purity. This faithfulness is expressed in our actions, such as faithful, lifelong commitment to our husband or wife. God intended marriage to be for life. Because marriage is the physical and spiritual union of a man and woman, dire consequences come from breaking this commitment.

This session will examine the Seventh Commandment, which outlines how sexual immorality distorts the picture of the gospel and becomes a behavior-controlling idol. Through the gospel, we're forgiven of our disobedience and set free to live in purity so others may see the glory of God.

Over the next week, center your mind's attention and heart's affection on this notion: that God wants us to follow Him and be faithful in our relationships. Interact with the Scriptures, and be ready to interact with your small group.

Why Does God Forbid Adultery?

Do not commit adultery.
DEUTERONOMY 5:18

Following the Commandment forbidding murder is the one forbidding adultery. Look at the stark, black-and-white way the Commandment comes to us. There are several reasons in Scripture that explain why God forbids adultery. Let's look at and briefly touch on each one.

1. It goes against God's original design (see Gen. 2:24-25).

2. It destroys marriages and families (see 2 Sam. 11).

3. It damages the picture of the gospel (see Gal. 3:24; Eph. 5:25).

4. It's an expression of spiritual adultery (see Ps. 51:4).

The prohibition against adultery doesn't make sense until we understand God's original design for sexual expression within the confines of marriage (#1). From the beginning, God established a blueprint for the family. Adam and Eve together reflected the image of God in their relationship of trust and love.

In Genesis 2:24-25, we read: "This is why a man leaves his father and mother and bonds with his wife, and they become one flesh. Both the man and his wife were naked, yet felt no shame." God's design was for one man to be united with one woman as one flesh. And in the innocence and purity of the garden of Eden, they would live together naked and not feel any shame.

What are some passages in the Bible that extol the beauty and glory of sex within marriage?

The glorious picture of marital bliss in the garden was shattered by human sin. When the first couple sinned against God, they became separated from God (#2). The marriage covenant is still powerful, but because of sin, it's a fractured version of what God originally intended.

A well-known story of adultery in Scripture is King David and Bathsheba in 2 Samuel 11. Ignoring the fact that she was married to Uriah, David slept with her and she became pregnant.

Realizing he couldn't hide this, David had Uriah killed. David didn't get away with this act of cruelty. God's law was clear, and it was intended to guide His people to a joy-filled life.

> Have you or someone you know walked through the pain caused by adultery? What were the consequences of this sin?

> Why do you think immorality is treated so seriously in Scripture?

You may wonder what adultery has to do with the gospel (#3). In Galatians 3:24, Paul wrote that "the law … was our guardian until Christ, so that we could be justified by faith." If we apply this verse about the law in general to the specific law against adultery, we see that this Commandment (like a guardian) was meant to protect marriage. It protects the design of what God established from the beginning. It also protected marriage as a picture of the gospel. Paul wrote that husbands are to love their wives as Christ loved the church (see Eph. 5:25).

Physical adultery may be against a spouse, but there's always a spiritual component that's against God (#4). That's why David, who sinned against Bathsheba and her husband, when confessing his sin, cried out to God for forgiveness (see Ps. 51:4). Physical adultery is an expression of spiritual adultery. In Scripture, God often describes His relationship with His people in terms of a marriage covenant. The expectation is love and fidelity. God is faithful and constantly pursuing His people, but His people "cheat" on Him by running after idols.

As believers, our relationship with Christ is now described in terms of a bride and groom. In James 4:4, we read that friendship with the world is hostility toward God. Those who give themselves over to worldly patterns of thought and behavior are "adulteresses"—serious language from a God serious about loving His people!

> What are some activities the Scriptures would consider spiritually adulterous toward God?

> In what ways can those of us who are single bring honor and glory to God in a way that displays the beauty of the gospel?

What are the Consequences?

We've seen that God forbids adultery because it unravels a bond that should never be broken. Now let's look at the consequences that come from disregarding the Seventh Commandment. Proverbs 6 gives instruction and warning against adultery.

> [20] My son, keep your father's command,
> and don't reject your mother's teaching.
> [21] Always bind them to your heart;
> tie them around your neck.
> [22] When you walk here and there, they will guide you;
> when you lie down, they will watch over you;
> when you wake up, they will talk to you.
> [23] For a command is a lamp, teaching is a light,
> and corrective discipline is the way to life.
> [24] They will protect you from an evil woman,
> from the flattering tongue of a stranger.
> [25] Don't lust in your heart for her beauty
> or let her captivate you with her eyelashes.
> [26] For a prostitute's fee is only a loaf of brad,
> but an adulteress goes after a precious life.
> [27] Can a man embrace fire
> and his clothes not be burned?
> [28] Can a man walk on burning coals
> without scorching his feet?
> [29] So it is with the one who sleeps with another man's wife;
> no one who touches her will go unpunished.
> PROVERBS 6:20-29

This passage begins with the author stating that his wisdom will bring life and discipline. It's written from the perspective of a father giving advice to his son. He wants him to stay away from the woman who has a flattering tongue. He warns his son not to lust after her or be captivated by her eyelashes. Notice the progression: flattery leads to lust and then infatuation.

What are some elements of temptation that can lead a person into sexual immorality?

In what ways can we guard against potentially compromising situations?

Do you see the contrast between life and death in Proverbs 6? The command to discipline oneself to stay away from adultery is "the way to life" (6:23). Obedience lends protection from evil and resistance to flattery (6:24). The adulteress goes after "a precious life" (6:36). Then note the imagery at the end: fire, burnt clothes, and scorched feet—vivid illustrations of the punishment promised in verse 29.

What are some examples of movies or television shows that romanticize or glamorize adultery? What should be our response to their message?

The consequences of adultery, just like the consequences of sin, are spiritual and physical death. If left unchecked, sexual desire can become an idol that consumes our hearts. That's why we must guard our heart from anything that would hinder our relationship with God. Choosing to disobey God is choosing death over life. Another consequence of adultery is that it cheapens the beautiful gift of sex that God has given us. The Bible doesn't just give us warnings about sex outside of marriage; it also commends sex inside of marriage. For example, Song of Solomon is a love poem between a husband and wife who have a strong physical and emotional desire for each other. They describe their physical attraction in vivid language. Take the beautiful descriptions of marital love in Song of Solomon and compare them to the warnings against adultery in Proverbs 6–7. Immediately you can see how sex outside of God's plan cheapens the gift.

In what ways can sexual sin become an idol? What are some ways you see a cheapening of sexuality in society today?

What are some various activities that would fall under the prohibition against adultery in the Seventh Commandment?

35

3 What is the Solution to a Lustful Heart?

We've seen that the prohibition against adultery is an expression of God's desire for His people to live according to His design. We've also seen that keeping this Commandment leads to life, while breaking this Commandment leads to death and destruction. We know that adultery tramples on the gift of marriage by polluting it with sexual immorality. But how do we stay pure? In a fallen world, we will battle lust and temptation. What do we do?

The law focuses on the action of what not to do. Jesus, however, went even further. Knowing that our actions and motives are marred by sin, Jesus claimed that even if we don't outwardly commit the sin of adultery, we're guilty because of our inward lusts. In Matthew 5, Jesus took the Seventh Commandment and went beyond the action to the heart.

> [27] You have heard that it was said, Do not commit adultery. [28] But I tell you, everyone who looks at a woman to lust for her has already committed adultery with her in his heart. [29] If your right eye causes you to sin, gouge it out and throw it away. For it is better that you lose one of the parts of your body than for your whole body to be thrown in hell. [30] And if your right hand causes you to sin, cut it off and throw it away. For it is better that you lose one of the parts of your body than for your whole body to go into hell!
>
> MATTHEW 5:27-30

According to Jesus, it's not the hands and feet that lead us to adultery; it's the heart. Therefore, the solution to a lustful heart isn't willpower or self-discipline. It's a heart transformation. The only solution to an adulterous heart is to have our hearts changed by the gospel. Living in light of this change, we are to do whatever it takes to remain pure.

How do we apply Jesus' teaching in this passage? We ought to recognize pornography as a form of adultery of the heart, just as lustful thoughts and fantasies are. Whether in the form of visual pictures or erotic romance novels, pornography leads to more and more lust. As those who have had our hearts transformed, we're called by Christ to go beyond the mere avoidance of adulterous actions and fight against adulterous thoughts as well. This may mean giving up some of the movies and television shows we watch. It may mean building in accountability online or on our phones. If that seems too severe, just look at the severity of Jesus' warnings in verses 29-30. Better to lose something that leads us to sin rather than be thrown in hell!

Proactively dealing with sexual sin and temptation doesn't mean creating a checklist of legalistic requirements. It means our pursuit of pleasure in God is greater than our pursuit of pleasure in the world. So take a good look at your life. If you are currently in or close to an adulterous relationship, end it immediately and confess. If you are addicted to Internet pornography, get some accountability. There should be urgency in fighting sexual sin.

How does pornography distort sexual desire?

What are some practical ways we can hold one another accountable as we seek to live holy, pure lives that glorify God?

In John 8, a group of scribes and Pharisees brought a woman caught in the act of adultery to Jesus. Would they stone her? Would Jesus consent to her death? Jesus told them that whoever was without sin should cast the first stone, and the men walked away. The implication was this—only Jesus had the right to stone the woman for her adultery. But did He? No. He didn't condemn her but instead told her to go and sin no more. She was forgiven, and we can be, too. She received the grace that only comes from Jesus, which empowered her to leave her life of sin.

How can we demonstrate the attitude of Christ toward those who have fallen into adultery?

How does the gospel give us hope as we deal with sexual sin?

GROUP STUDY

Warm Up

There are a number of different detective shows on television. From *Law & Order* to *CSI*, people love television shows that start with a crime and then tell the story of motive. The motive and the action go hand-in-hand. The mystery is in finding out who is guilty and why they committed the crime. Internal motives lead to external actions.

Christ was interested in motives as well. One time while addressing a crowd, Jesus explained the Seventh Commandment in more detail (see Matt. 5:27-28). It wasn't just about the action of adultery, but also the lust that leads to adultery. By making it a heart issue, Jesus was raising the bar.

In connecting adultery to lust, Jesus was laying out a view of the law that goes back to the heart. This would be the new order of things. This would be how His followers would know one another. Not just by external behaviors and prohibitions but by inward transformation.

> ³ For though we live in the world, we do not wage war as the world does.
> ⁴ The weapons we fight with are not the weapons of the world. On the contrary, they have divine power to demolish strongholds. ⁵ We demolish arguments and every pretension that sets itself up against the knowledge of God, and we take captive every thought to make it obedient to Christ. ⁶ And we will be ready to punish every act of disobedience, once your obedience is complete.
> **2 CORINTHIANS 10:3-6**

The law against adultery makes us think, *I need to change my behavior.* But Jesus' explanation of that law makes us think, *I need a new heart!* And that's what God gives us through Jesus' death and resurrection. Now, as believers redeemed by Christ's blood, we are freed from the slavery of lust and sin.

How will you take every thought captive to obey Christ?

In what ways do you bring your motives in submission to Christ?

Discussion

The church is supposed to be different from the world. Jesus said in Matthew 5 that we're to be the light of the world. Our attitudes and actions should be different from those outside the church. We demonstrate the beauty of godly living, not by lording our morals over others but by showing them the wisdom of following Christ and the grace of trusting Him for forgiveness. The stronger our marriages, the stronger our gospel witness.

Use this time to share what God has revealed as you connect the dots and pursue the gospel. Some of the questions below are from your daily reading assignments. They will guide your small-group discussion.

1. How do you measure your faithfulness to those important to you—friends, family, parents, spouse, co-workers, boss?

2. Have you or someone you know walked through the pain caused by adultery? What were the consequences of this sin?

3. What are some activities the Scriptures would consider spiritually adulterous toward God?

4. In what ways can those of us who are single bring honor and glory to God in a way that displays the beauty of the gospel?

5. What are some elements of temptation that can lead a person into sexual immorality? In what ways can we guard against potentially compromising situations?

6. In what ways can sexual sin become an idol? What are some ways you see a cheapening of sexuality in society today?

7. How can we demonstrate the attitude of Christ toward those who have fallen into adultery? How does the gospel give us hope as we deal with sexual sin?

Conclusion

Have you ever driven down a highway at night and seen a city from a distance? It can be a beautiful sight. In the lone desert, Las Vegas stands out. The bright lights in the dark vast space of desert make the city look like a star when seen from an airplane. If you were to place Las Vegas on a high hill rather than a flat landscape, it would be even more visible than it is already.

In Matthew 5:14-16, Jesus said we should let our light shine before men so that they may see our good works. Our faith should transform us into people who do good works. Our works in turn will act as the shining light. The light transforms the darkness. It can be seen from a distance.

Spend some time praying this for you and for your group:

"God, I want to be a shining light for You. Help me to reach the darkness with the love of Your light. Help me to remain faithful to You and to my spouse. Use us as a picture of Your love for the world. Amen."

1. Eric Mason, *Manhood Restored* (Nashville: B&H, 2013), 92-93.
2. Martin Luther, The Small Catechism, in *The Reformation Reader*, ed. Denis Janz (Minneapolis: Fortress Press, 1999), 114.

We should fear and love God, and so we should lead
a chaste and pure life in word and deed, each one
loving and honoring his wife or her husband.[2]

MARTIN LUTHER

NOTES

THE GOSPEL PROJECT

Session 4

Our Relationship with Possessions

The eighth commandment isn't just about stealing; it's also about stewardship.[1]

PHILIP GRAHAM RYKEN

INDIVIDUAL STUDY

At the turn of the millennium, a debate about technology and ethics began over something many would consider a minor offense. Shawn Fanning, John Fanning, and Sean Parker formed a program enabling computers to share files. They called it Napster®. The program allowed users to share media across the Internet through a peer-to-peer network—giving birth to the phenomenon of illegally downloading music and movies.

Within months, teenagers who had computers and high-speed connections could bypass music stores and download songs from one another and save them to CDs. Many of you reading this probably used similar file-sharing services at some point in the past.

Eventually musicians filed lawsuits against Napster for illegally spreading music throughout the world. The people who created Napster and the people who used it suddenly found themselves in trouble as the government began investigating and fining file-sharers.[2]

The rise and fall of Napster raises some questions about stealing. What does it mean to commit theft? Why does God condemn stealing? Should we only be worried about stealing that has legal consequences? Does the enforcement of the law matter? Questions like these take us back to the Scriptures, where God commanded His people to not steal.

> Can you recall a time when you stole something from someone?

> Has someone stolen something from you? What was the situation, and what did you learn?

In the Eighth Commandment, God forbids stealing—taking something that doesn't belong to us. In this session, we'll see that this Commandment covers a wide range of dishonest practices birthed in a heart gripped by possessions instead of the One from whom all good things come. Because of Christ, we're set free from our slavery to things and are given new, generous hearts that aid us in our mission.

Throughout the week engage these daily study sections on your own. Each of these readings revolves around a different aspect of the Eighth Commandment—do not steal. They will help you prepare for your small-group discussion. Interact with the Scriptures, and be ready to interact with your small group.

1 Why Does God Forbid Stealing?

As we've seen in previous sessions, the Ten Commandments come within a story—the history of God's redemption of His people. Within the context of His saving acts, God issued this command intended to help His people live in community:

Do not steal.
DEUTERONOMY 5:19

Why was this Commandment necessary? Why do we have to be taught not to steal? To start with, stealing comes from a covetous heart. (We will cover the Commandment against coveting in an upcoming session.)

The word *covet* isn't common in our vernacular, but it means to desire something that doesn't belong to us. In a world loaded with advertising at every turn, it's easy to focus on the items we don't have or can't afford. Commercials for cars, fashion, and electronics tell us that we can have a better life by owning new products. The items themselves may not be evil, but how we feel about what we don't yet have is where the struggle lies.

Stealing is the evidence of our covetous nature. It begins as a desire in our mind, and then it results in the action of taking something that doesn't belong to us. James 1 breaks down the process of temptation and sin, telling us that each man is drawn by his own desire. It's the sinful desire within us that leads us to covet and eventually steal.

Why does God condemn both stealing and coveting? What is the connection between the two?

How can we loosen the grip of possessions in our life?

How early in life do children demonstrate coveting and stealing? Is such behavior taught or does it come naturally?

At its core, stealing is idolatrous. It disregards the law of God for our own personal gain. It's a sign that we are placing our desires above His commands. In this way, we've become our own god.

Breaking this command demonstrates what we truly value. Our desire for money or possessions exceeds our desire for God when we choose to violate His law in order to get what we want. When we take something that isn't ours, we demonstrate our failure to love God completely. Stealing says, "The object of my desire will satisfy my needs more than God." Stealing says, "I don't trust God to provide for me."

Another reason God forbids stealing is that this sin strikes at the heart of an important truth—God owns everything. We are merely managers of what God has given us. What we have comes from Him and still ultimately belongs to Him. Stealing isn't just taking something that doesn't belong to us; it's robbing God of the glory that's His.

This is why Jesus told His disciples not to worry about their food, shelter, or clothing (see Matt. 6). If God cares for the birds and flowers, how much more will He care for His people! Theft begins in the covetous heart that desires something more than God, or it's the manifestation of a faithless heart that fails to see all good things as coming from God.

Can we consider improper stewardship of God's gifts a form of stealing? Why or why not?

What are some things we try to find satisfaction in apart from God?

Why is stealing someone else's belongings an offense against God?

2 Stealing Extends to Dishonest Dealings

Stealing isn't just robbing a bank or shoplifting in a store. There are many forms of theft, and all are sins before God. For example:

> 13 "You must not have two different weights in your bag, one heavy
> and one light. 14 You must not have two differing dry measures in
> your house, a larger and a smaller. 15 You must have a full and honest
> weight, a full and honest dry measure, so that you may live long in
> the land the LORD your God is giving you. 16 For everyone who does
> such things and acts unfairly is detestable to the LORD your God.
> **DEUTERONOMY 25:13-16**

In this passage, we see that dishonest scales (measuring things heavier when you sell or lighter when you buy) are condemned. So stealing applies to more than theft of someone's belongings; it's also a matter of trust. For example, when you write a check to someone, they're trusting in you to have sufficient funds in your account to cover the expense. Thus, stealing isn't only connected to coveting (the Tenth Commandment) but also to lying (the Ninth Commandment).

What are some examples of stealing non-monetary items? What kinds of stealing do people in society overlook or accept?

Here are some examples of stealing disgusted as "dishonest dealings":

Withholding Wages. Many times in the Old and New Testaments, we find God condemning injustice in all of its forms. Those who exploit their workers for personal gain aren't only accountable to society but also to God. We who follow Jesus should beware of becoming bosses, supervisors, or CEOs who countenance unfairness.

For those of you who are managers and supervisors, you need to pay workers the wages and overtime they've earned. Don't make promises that can't be kept; instead, be a person who fulfills your word. By doing so, you're not just honoring your employees but honoring God as well.

Clocked-out while clocked-in. Time is money in the workplace. When we're not giving our full attention or effort at our jobs, we're stealing company time. It doesn't matter whether you're paid by yearly salary or contracted hourly, you can be sure that God desires for you to give your all in your work. As Colossians 3:23-24 tells us, "Whatever you do, do it enthusiastically, as something done for the Lord and not for men, knowing that you will receive the reward of an inheritance from the Lord. You serve the Lord Christ." We must refuse the urge to cheat our bosses or companies by being "clocked out" mentally while "clocked in" physically.

In what ways can you become a better steward of the things God has given you (possessions, time, gifts, talents, authority, employee responsibility)?

Paying Government Taxes. Another example of stealing is to employ dishonest means in order to pay as little tax as possible. Like them or not, taxes are intended to provide services for the community, including salaries for government officials, policemen, firemen, and teachers. By failing to report properly on our tax forms, we steal money out of the budgets that help our communities run properly. This is an example of a sin that has direct consequences on the community as a whole.

Plagiarism. As mentioned at the beginning of the lesson, stealing music over the Internet has led to the illegal global sharing of information. Plagiarism isn't just stealing but also lying (which is forbidden in the Ninth Commandment). This activity gives a false perception that you created something when in fact someone else did. If you're guilty of plagiarism, then you're stealing credit for someone else's work. This would include hiring someone else to write a paper or buying a paper written by someone else. This kind of dishonesty shows up in different forms, and it can create ethical dilemmas for followers of Christ. Understanding what the Bible teaches about dishonesty and its relationship to theft, we should be a people who conform to what the Bible teaches.

What other ways do you see "dishonest dealings" at work, home, school, or in the community?

Have you ever been guilty of these types of theft? If so, which ones?

At what point did you realize this was stealing? What steps did you take to make it right?

3 Become "Givers," Not "Takers"

In ancient times, the punishment for stealing could be quite harsh. Many a man lost an arm or hand for taking something forbidden. Horrible punishments may be one way to deter thievery, but they don't change the heart. Only Jesus can deliver us from the desire to take what doesn't belong to us. And when He does, He replaces it with the desire to give.

When we follow Jesus, we're gradually transformed from selfish to generous. We become less concerned with material wealth and more concerned with treasures in heaven. Our mindset on wealth changes from hoarding possessions for our own desires to using possessions as a tool to advance the kingdom of God. Whether we're giving to our church, supporting righteous causes, or helping the poor, our money can serve as a great example of how the gospel has changed us.

The Gospel of Luke gives insight into how Christ can change our selfishness to generosity. As Jesus was journeying to Jericho, He stopped to acknowledge a man named Zacchaeus:

> [1] He entered Jericho and was passing through. [2] There was a man named Zacchaeus who was a chief tax collector, and he was rich. [3] He was trying to see who Jesus was, but he was not able because of the crowd, since he was a short man. [4] So running ahead, he climbed up a sycamore tree to see Jesus, since He was about to pass that way. [5] When Jesus came to the place, He looked up and said to him, "Zacchaeus, hurry and come down because today I must stay at your house." [6] So he quickly came down and welcomed Him joyfully. [7] All who saw it began to complain, "He's gone to lodge with a sinful man!" [8] But Zacchaeus stood there and said to the Lord, "Look, I'll give half of my possessions to the poor, Lord! And if I have extorted anything from anyone, I'll pay back four times as much!" [9] "Today salvation has come to this house," Jesus told him, "because he too is a son of Abraham. [10] For the Son of Man has come to seek and to save the lost."
>
> LUKE 19:1-10

At the beginning of the story, we know three things about Zacchaeus—he was a chief tax collector, he was rich, and he was short. Tax collectors at this time were viewed as thieves because they charged the people more than what they owed. Zacchaeus must have done well for himself considering the author mentioned that he was rich. After meeting Jesus in a very humiliating way, he was quick to respond with joy. He offered to give half of his possessions to the poor and pay back those whom he extorted at an exorbitant interest rate. His change of heart was immediately evident.

How does our generosity reflect the gospel?

Using Zacchaeus as an example, we can see how stinginess is a sign that we don't know the grace of God. Grace isn't fairness. Grace isn't a karmic state that allows us to repay God for the wonderful acts that He has done for us. Grace is receiving something that we could never deserve. We are saved by grace through faith because we couldn't accomplish it on our own.

This is what Ephesians 2:8-9 tells us: "For you are saved by grace through faith, and this is not from yourselves; it is God's gift—not from works, so that no one can boast." Grace prohibits us from boasting because we couldn't accomplish our own salvation. If we could save ourselves, then it would never have been grace.

Grace is what we experience on our end of salvation, but generosity is what God demonstrates on His. Because our sin was a debt that was so great, it took a God who was rich in mercy to pay for our deficit. The payment would be the life of His Son so that we could experience life for eternity. This is the highest payment that anyone could give.

Ephesians 2:4 tells us that He did so because of His great love for us. Generosity is rooted in a selfless love for others. We demonstrate love by being generous, but we can't truly be generous without love. Jesus once told His disciples, "No one has greater love than this, that someone would lay down his life for his friends" (John 15:13). In laying down His life, Jesus demonstrated the ultimate form of generosity that was rooted in love.

Do you agree with Jesus' words that "it is more blessed to give than to receive" (Acts 20:35)? How can your life display your belief in this truth?

Describe a time when the gospel motivated you to "give" rather than "take." How did this experience bless others? Glorify God? Make much of the gospel?

GROUP STUDY

Warm Up

Read these quotes about stealing, honesty, and possessions as you begin your discussion.

Where Faith begins, anxiety ends; Where
anxiety begins, Faith ends.[3]
GEORGE MÜLLER (1805-1898)

[Jesus'] believers should not see any of their
money as their own, and they should be profoundly
involved with and generous to the poor.[4]
TIMOTHY KELLER

When someone steals, we all pay for it.[5]
J. ELLSWORTH KALAS

The world's ethic is marked by taking, not giving. But the
church can step in here and become an alternative society.
We can be a lifesaver for a culture drowning in thievery.[6]
TULLIAN TCHIVIDJIAN

Which quote resonates with you the most? Why?

Why do you think stealing transcend time and culture? What do you see
is the common thread woven throughout these quotes?

Sin can disguise itself within the desires that already reside within us all. This notion runs contrary to the idea that we're inherently good and that temptation is just an external issue. James 1:14 says, "But each person is tempted when he is drawn away and enticed by his own evil desires." The Holy Spirit helps us counteract our evil desires so we aren't drawn into sin. The temptation remains because the flesh is still part of us for now. But we also have a Helper to deal with it. The same power that raised Jesus Christ from the dead is the same power that will help us overcome sin, flesh, temptation, and the Enemy.

Discussion

Changing our actions doesn't necessarily reflect a true change in heart. TV reality show *The Biggest Loser* (Season 3) winner was Erik Chopin. He began the competition weighing in at 407 pounds and finished at 193 pounds! His amazing transformation was due to his hard work with the help of his trainer. However, Erik returned home to the same set of circumstances that made him obese prior to the competition. He went back up to 302 pounds. The change on the outside was because of the external factors. But Erik didn't change his mind and heart about food and its role in his life. Erik re-entered the competition and lost the weight again.

This is a good picture and analogy of true repentance and the power of the gospel to transform hearts. Use this time to share what God has revealed as you over the week. Some of the questions below are from your daily reading assignments. They will guide your small-group discussion.

1. Why does God condemn both stealing and coveting? What is the connection between the two? How can we loosen the grip of possessions in our life?

2. How early in life do children demonstrate coveting and stealing? Is such behavior taught or does it come naturally?

3. Can we consider improper stewardship of God's gifts a form of stealing? Why or why not? What are some things we try to find satisfaction in apart from God?

4. In your own words, why is stealing someone else's belongings considered an offense against God?

5. How do we participate in "dishonest dealings" (stealing) at work, home, school, or in the community? What kinds of stealing do people in society overlook or accept?

6. How does our generosity reflect the gospel? When our hearts are not in the right place, is it better to give begrudgingly or not give at all?

7. Do you agree with Jesus' words that "it is more blessed to give than to receive" (Acts 20:35)? How does your life reflect this truth?

Conclusion

Ephesians 4:28 gives us a glimpse into what repentance looks like for anyone else who steals. It says, "The thief must no longer steal. Instead, he must do honest work with his own hands, so that he has something to share with anyone in need." The heart that was once focused on self is now focused on others. This is what the gospel does. This is what the "good news" sounds like to a heart consumed with greed.

In the same way, each one of us is to make sure that our focus is not on ourselves but on God and others. We should resemble Christ, who didn't steal anything but freely gave all He had generously out of love and obedience to God.

Spend some time praying this for you and for your group:

> "God, help me follow Jesus into a life of generosity. Use me to show the world how generous You are! My possessions are a means to a greater end. Use them so others can hear and see the gospel. Amen."

1. Philip Graham Ryken, *Written in Stone*, 174.
2. Tom Lamont, "Napster: the day the music was set free" *The Guardian,* February 23, 2013, Online *http://www.theguardian.com/music/2013/feb/24/napster-music-free-file-sharing*
3. George Müller, quoted in *George Muller of Bristol*, by A. T. Pierson (Waymark Books, 2010), 226.
4. Timothy Keller, *Generous Justice* (New York: Riverhead, 2010), 49
5. J. Ellsworth Kalas, *The Ten Commandments from the Back Side* (Nashville: Abingdon Press, 1998), 83.
6. Tullian Tchividjian, *Unfashionable: Making a Difference in the World by Being Different* (Colorado Springs: Multnomah Books, 2009), 129.
7. St. Maximus of Turin, Sermon 95, *The Sermons of St. Maximus of Turin*, trans. Boniface Ramsey, quoted in *Ancient Christian Writers*, issue 50 (Paulist Press, 1989), 219.

There is no crime in possessions, but there is crime in those who do not know how to use possessions. For the foolish, wealth is a temptation to vice, but for the wise, it is a help to virtue.[7]

MAXIMUS OF TURIN (380-465)

NOTES

THE GOSPEL PROJECT

Session 5

Our Relationship with the Truth

And then she understood the devilish cunning of the enemies' plan.
By mixing a little truth with it they had made their lie far stronger.[1]

C.S. LEWIS

INDIVIDUAL STUDY

During the 2000 Summer Olympic Games, Marion Jones became a household name as she brought honor to her country. She won a record five medals at the Olympiad—three gold and two bronze. Her performance was astonishing as she demonstrated dominance in the sport of track and field that many had never seen. Jones would receive wealth and fame as a result of her victories. She endorsed companies like Nike® and Gatorade®. She was the hope and promise of athleticism in the United States for about five years.

But then rumors surfaced about her use of performance-enhancing drugs. Jones testified to federal agents while under oath that she was not guilty of using steroids. She would not relent from her pursuit of a drug-free image. But Jones was convicted of perjury and sentenced to six months in prison. Subsequently, she was stripped of all her Olympic medals. All of her hard work, training, and competing would be undone. She also found herself in financial trouble and participated in a check fraud scheme. This was yet another lie. For her, this wasn't a one-time offense. And although Jones has the chance to redeem her reputation and livelihood moving forward, lying destroyed part of the life she built for herself.

What are some examples of the destructive power of lies?

Lies seem simple. They seem harmless. They may even seem necessary to protect what is important. Some would say certain types of lies are permissible. But we need to be careful that we don't deceive ourselves in deceiving others. God's Word is truth, and God encourages us to be a people of truth as well.

In the Ninth Commandment, God forbids us to bear false witness against our neighbors. Throughout the Old Testament, He expressed His hatred for lying lips and declared truthfulness to be a requirement for His people. Jesus was falsely accused for our sake. But because of Him, we can be forgiven when we repent (tell the truth about ourselves) and believe the gospel (believe the truth about Jesus). As a truth-telling people, the church now bears a true witness to Christ.

Throughout the week engage these daily study sections on your own. Each of these readings revolves around a different aspect of the Ninth Commandment, and they will help you prepare for your small-group discussion. Interact with the Scriptures, and be ready to interact with your small group.

Why Does God Forbid Lying?

Do not give dishonest testimony against your neighbor.
DEUTERONOMY 5:20

The first thing we need to know about lying is the specific command from God against giving a false testimony—we shouldn't lie to others. No exceptions are given. We're simply told to obey. However, the law does get specific about certain types of lying in Exodus 23.

[1] You must not spread a false report. Do not join
the wicked to be a malicious witness.
[2] You must not follow a crowd in wrongdoing. Do not testify
in a lawsuit and go along with a crowd to pervert justice. [3] Do
not show favoritism to a poor person in his lawsuit.
EXODUS 23:1-3

We live in a world that makes money off the lies this passage speaks against. Tabloids lie about celebrities and politicians, and an entire wing of the entertainment industry has been built on the backs of lies that appear as news. As believers, we must seek out the truth and learn to discern the difference between news and gossip.

What kinds of lies are seen as culturally acceptable today? How should Christians respond to gossip in the church?

Here are some forms of lying we must watch out for:

Stretching the truth. One form is embellishment. Sometimes this is meant in fun during the telling of a story by making the surrounding details more exaggerated than they truly are. However, this can also be done in a malicious manner to tear down someone's reputation. As Christians, we should make sure that when asked to give an account of a situation, we're not embellishing details that could change the outcome of a person's punishment or reward.

White lies. Another popular way to lie is the concept of white lies. White lies are seen as minor and harmless, often used to shelter someone from a hurtful truth. White lies may seem innocent, but even the innocence is deceptive. We lie first to ourselves in telling a white lie. Yes, believers should be encouraging, but we should also tell the truth in love. Proverbs 27:6

reminds us, "The wounds of a friend are trustworthy, but the kisses of an enemy are excessive." A true friend will tell us the truth at all times, even when it hurts.

Intentional deception. One more type of lie is intentional deception—an explicit disregard for the truth in order to convince someone of a falsehood. For example, Jacob, the second-born son of Isaac, deceived his father in order to receive the blessing of the firstborn (see Gen. 27). Esau was so angry that he vowed to kill his brother, and Jacob was forced to flee from his family. An intentional deception to create a desired scenario tore this family apart.

> When have you witness lying tearing a family apart? How can we cultivate truth-telling in our homes and churches?

Lies can have severe consequences, especially in matters of justice. Therefore, God warned leaders to make sure their dealings with people were honest. Examine Exodus 23:6-8:

> [6] You must not deny justice to a poor person among you in his lawsuit.
> [7] Stay far away from a false accusation. Do not kill the innocent and the just, because I will not justify the guilty. [8] You must not take a bribe, for a bribe blinds the clear-sighted and corrupts the words of the righteous.
> EXODUS 23:6-8

Everyone who serves in government is ultimately responsible to God, for Romans 13 says God is the One who sets the governing authorities over us. But Christ followers must hear this instruction from the Book of Exodus as well, and fight injustice in all its forms. In all of this, Paul reminded us in Philippians 2 that our attitude should resemble Christ's. Even though He was God, He chose not to lord this fact over us. He humbled Himself, served others, and died on a cross. Likewise, we need to seek out the interests of others by telling them the truth in love.

> What do you think are the most common lies people tell themselves? Why should we be aware of our motives to lie?

> How can we practically resist temptation to lie?

2 A Truthful Heart is Required

God didn't create us for lies but for truth. Throughout Scripture, God declares His hatred of lying. Psalm 5:6 says, "You destroy those who tell lies." He is against those who choose to be dishonest. In Proverbs 6:16-19, Solomon told the things that God detests, and he mentioned lying twice: God hates a lying tongue and He detests a lying witness who gives a false report.

God makes it clear that He hates lying. So how do we reflect the nature of God on this point?

First John 2:4 tells us, "The one who says, 'I have come to know Him,' yet doesn't keep His commands, is a liar, and the truth is not in him." We demonstrate the truth in us by matching our actions with the commands of Christ. If we preach grace yet withhold forgiveness, then we deceive. If we claim to follow the Servant-King Jesus and yet choose to put our needs above the needs of others, then we lie.

Why does God take lying so seriously?

Do you think churches take lying seriously? Why or why not?

Idolatry (prohibited in the First and Second Commandments) is built on deception that something should come before God. Therefore, lies are a barrier to experiencing Jesus Christ. John 1:17 tells believers that grace and truth come from Jesus Christ. John 4:24 informs us that we should worship in spirit and in truth. Jesus told His disciples in John 14:6 that He is the way, the truth, and the life.

Truth and gospel go hand in hand. If we pursue lies, then we are avoiding the gospel completely. The Old Testament bears this out as well.

[1] LORD, who can dwell in Your tent?
Who can live on Your holy mountain?
[2] The one who lives honestly, practices righteousness,
and acknowledges the truth in his heart—
[3] who does not slander with his tongue,
who does not harm his friend
or discredit his neighbor,
[4] who despises the one rejected by the LORD
but honors those who fear the LORD
who keeps his word whatever the cost,
[5] who does not lend his money at interest
or take a bribe against the innocent—
the one who does these things will never be moved

PSALM 15:1-5

Psalm 15 was a prophetic psalm describing what the Messiah would be like, and the Messiah would be a person of integrity. One quality listed said he would be a person who "keeps his word whatever the cost." Who else but Jesus? While on trial in front of His false accusers, He could have denied His deity and taken the easy way out. He could have avoided isolation, persecution, and death by lying about who He was, but He chose to tell the truth.

When confronted by the Roman governor Pilate, Jesus said, "You say that I'm a king … I was born for this, and I have come into the world for this: to testify to the truth. Everyone who is of the truth listens to My voice" (John 18:37). Pilate tried to convince Jesus to recant, but He wouldn't. He's the Messiah and He couldn't deny the truth of His kingship and kingdom. He fulfilled the prophecy in Psalm 15, showing He would keep His word whatever the cost.

To what degree does your life communicate "honesty and integrity"?

What are the effects of dishonesty from a believer?

3 Put Away Lying and Put on the New Self

Because Christ serves as our example of truth embodied, we need to put away any practice of lying.

> [9] Do not lie to one another, since you have put off the old self with its practices [10] and have put on the new self. You are being renewed in knowledge according to the image of your Creator.
> COLOSSIANS 3:9-10

Honesty is a primary indicator of the change that has taken place in Christians. Because we have the truth of the gospel and a new identity in Christ, we should be truthful with one another and toward God. Yet this is only possible because the Holy Spirit empowers us to put away the "old self" and embrace the "new self." Jesus told His disciples that the Holy Spirit is the "Spirit of truth" and that He would be with us forever (see John 14:17). Believers don't need to fear the truth because we have the Spirit of truth living inside of us.

We have been called to make disciples from all nations. We can't go into the world and expect them to believe our message unless we walk in the truth. In order to reach a world that has been deceived by sin, we need to make sure we live a life of integrity. Our lives need to match our message.

Think about a time when the Holy Spirit led you into truth about a certain situation. What were the circumstances?

How did the Holy Spirit reveal the truth and resonate with your spirit?

How have you experienced the "new life" in Christ? Explain the difference you see in your walk and talk, action and attitude.

Contrast all of this with what Jesus said about Satan and his children in John 8:42-47:

> [42] Jesus said to them, "If God were your Father, you would love Me, because I came from God and I am here. For I didn't come on My own, but He sent Me. [43] Why don't you understand what I say? Because you cannot listen to My word. [44] You are of your father the Devil, and you want to carry out your father's desires. He was a murderer from the beginning and has not stood in the truth, because there is no truth in him. When he tells a lie, he speaks from his own nature, because he is a liar and the father of liars. [45] Yet because I tell the truth, you do not believe Me. [46] Who among you can convict Me of sin? If I tell the truth, why don't you believe Me? [47] The one who is from God listens to God's words. This is why you don't listen, because you are not from God."

Jesus' sharp statements in this passage show how serious He was about dealing with the Pharisees on the subject of truth and lies. They constantly made false accusations against Him, and yet He countered them with the truth. He told them they were just like their father, the Devil, calling Him a murderer and a liar by nature. So those who deny Christ also speak from a lying nature, being children of the Devil. Christians, on the other hand, are different from who we were before Christ because our identity is now found in Him.

How does honesty aid you in your mission to share the truth of Jesus Christ?

GROUP STUDY

Warm Up

Metamorphosis is a process. Consider the journey of a butterfly. An egg hatches into a larva, more commonly known as a caterpillar. The caterpillar eats leaves and grows stronger. The larva eventually develops into a pupa, also known as the cocoon. The cocoon is where the caterpillar's body rests, grows, and changes. The change takes place over a different period of time. And each season of change is different for each butterfly. Eventually the butterfly outgrows the cocoon and emerges ready to fly.

But once a butterfly emerges from its cocoon, it doesn't attempt to climb back into it. It doesn't seek to exist as a caterpillar. It doesn't desire to live "a simpler life" as an egg. Instead, it moves forward—naturally, progressively.

Read Ephesians 4:20-24.

> [20] But that is not how you learned about the Messiah, [21] assuming you heard about Him and were taught by Him, because the truth is in Jesus. [22] You took off your former way of life, the old self that is corrupted by deceitful desires; [23] you are being renewed in the spirit of your minds; [24] you put on the new self, the one created according to God's likeness in righteousness and purity of the truth.

How are you moving forward with your "new identity" in Christ?

In what ways has God taught you how to "shed" your past to embrace the next stage of your spiritual growth?

What is next for you on your journey?

Once we have turned from our sin and are alive in Christ, we shouldn't intentionally seek out sin. Paul addresses the fact that believers shouldn't lie to one another because they have put off the old self with old practices and have put on an entirely new self. We shouldn't willingly lie to one another anymore. That part of our life is done! If you're in Christ, stay turned from sin and don't seek out the sin of the past. We're renewed in knowledge according to the image of God.

Discussion

Jesus Christ embodied the truth, and because we're being made like Christ through the work of the Holy Spirit, we too should embody the truth. We've put off this old self and put on the new self through faith in Christ. Now we're being renewed daily according to the image of our Creator, who is the God of truth. Live the truth of who you are in Christ, and speak the truth of what God has done for us in Christ. Listed below are some of the questions from your daily reading assignments. They will guide your small-group discussion.

1. What kinds of lies are seen as culturally acceptable today? How should Christians respond to gossip in the church?

2. When have you witnessed lying tearing a family apart? How can we cultivate truth-telling in our homes and churches?

3. Why do you think God takes lying so seriously? Do you think churches take lying seriously? Why or why not?

4. To what degree does your life communicate "honesty and integrity"? What are the effects of dishonesty from a believer?

5. Think about a time when the Holy Spirit led you into truth about a certain situation. What were the circumstances? How did the Holy Spirit reveal the truth and resonate with your spirit?

6. How have you experienced the "new life" in Christ? Explain the difference you see in your walk and talk, action and attitude.

7. How does honesty aid you in your mission to share the truth of Jesus Christ?

Conclusion

We need to be aware that our integrity can affect our ability to share the gospel. Because we know the ultimate truth, it's important that we're known as people who don't lie. We should strive to be truthful in all of our dealings so we're above reproach when we speak with others.

In the same way that Christ told the truth about Himself, we too must tell the truth about Christ and the salvation He offers. In response to Christ's work, we repent by faith. In this we agree with Jesus and tell the truth about ourselves. We admit we are sinners, and our sin is in violation of God's law. But we believe the truth about Jesus. We confess the truth of His deity and His death, burial, and resurrection. Honesty is essential for true followers of Jesus as we believe and preach the truth of the gospel.

Spend some time praying this for you and for your group:

> "God, help me find my way in Jesus Christ. I seek to live and obey
> Your commands. Jesus, You are the way, the truth, and the life. Thank
> You for Your gospel. Help me reflect this to those around me."

1..C. S. Lewis, *The Last Battle* (New York: HarperCollins, 1984), 127.
2. Timothy Keller, *Generous Justice* (New York: Riverhead, 2010), 49.

[Jesus'] believers should not see any of their money as their own, and they should be profoundly involved with and generous to the poor.[2]

TIMOTHY KELLER

NOTES

Session 6

Our Relationship with Our Desires

The greedy person—one who covets—denies
his faith in God and scorns His values.[1]
Williams J. Fallis

INDIVIDUAL STUDY

Coveting is a sin more covert than most because it's almost exclusively an issue of the heart. Other sins are easy to discern through external actions, but coveting can be concealed. We may not even be conscious of how our covetous heart affects our relationship with others and with God. Ultimately, coveting speaks of our dissatisfaction with God and what He has done for us.

A movie that depicts the sin of coveting is *The Count of Monte Cristo*. It's based on the novel by Alexandre Dumas. In this classic, Edmond Dantes is betrayed by his friend, Fernand—fueled by his personal jealousy over Edmond's engagement to Mercedes. Fernand enacts a plot to accuse Edmond of being a traitor to his country, resulting in his banishment to a prison known as Chateau d'If. Fernand forsook his friend and destroyed his reputation all because he coveted what he could not have.

Like Fernand, we too can be consumed by the sin of coveting. Desiring what someone else has for our own satisfaction is a sin that can lead to disastrous consequences.

What does coveting look like? In your own words, how would you define it?

How concerned are you about the sin of coveting?

In this last and Tenth Commandment, God forbids us to covet something that belongs to someone else. Coveting is the craving of the heart for something we believe will give us satisfaction. Instead, coveting isolates us from others and robs us of a proper perspective of earthly things. The gospel is the only answer to covetousness, for only Jesus provides us with a way to find our satisfaction in God and His gifts. Through faith in Jesus, we're given new desires that are in line with God's mission.

Throughout the week engage these daily study sections on your own. Center your mind and heart on God's Word. Each of these readings revolves around a different aspect of the Tenth Commandment—do not covet. Interact with the Scriptures. They will guide your small-group discussion.

God Warns Against a Coveting Heart

Coveting is a sin that can't be policed because we can never see it on the outside. Much like the First Commandment, which commands us to worship God, coveting is played out primarily within the heart. It involves the misplaced cravings of the heart, and the Tenth Commandment lists different things that people shouldn't covet.

> Do not covet your neighbor's wife or desire your neighbor's house, his field, his male or female slave, his ox or donkey, or anything that belongs to your neighbor.
>
> DEUTERONOMY 5:21

Immediately we notice that God didn't stop with "Do not covet." Many of the other Commandments are simple, but this one gets specific for the sake of covering all the bases. Look at all the different things we aren't supposed to desire!

You shouldn't covet your neighbor's spouse. By avoiding this sin, you can avoid an adulterous relationship. You can also avoid breaking a relationship with your own spouse and your neighbor. Just the mere thoughts of desire can inspire jealously and anger on all sides of a relationship. Coveting is a dangerous sin.

You shouldn't covet anyone's possessions. In other words, we shouldn't be concerned with "keeping up" with anyone else. Perhaps we're familiar with coveting a neighbor's house or field, but coveting an ox or donkey for those who live in rural cultures also violates this command. And though not part of our context, it's clear that even the coveting of slaves could have been a temptation for the people of Israel.

You shouldn't covet anything. The command closes with a summary to include all things. We aren't supposed to covet anything that belongs to our neighbor. And the parable of the "Good Samaritan" found in Luke 10:25-37 teaches us that everyone is our neighbor. We aren't to covet anything from anyone.

How would the Tenth Commandment found in Deuteronomy 5:21 read in today's contemporary language and culture?

What would be comparable objects we covet?

At the heart of coveting is discontentment with God. He's the One who provides opportunities and supplies all of our needs. Everything that we have comes from His hand.

James 1:17 tells us, "Every generous act and every perfect gift is from above, coming down from the Father of lights; with Him there is no variation or shadow cast by turning." God is the true Provider of all that is good in our lives. He's the Creator who gives good and perfect gifts to His children. We aren't to look at the Father who has given us life and redemption and tell Him we're dissatisfied with what we have. We have already been given more than we deserve.

Coveting also destroys relationships with others. We become bitter toward those of whom we are envious, questioning why they have been given a blessing that we want for ourselves. This shows that coveting violates the entire law. We can't love God with our heart, soul, mind, and strength if we're angry about what He has given us. We can't love our neighbor if we're envious of what God has given them.

The simple truth is this: human desires are insatiable. We don't receive pleasures when we get what we want because we always find ourselves wanting more. It's fitting that the law mentions so many possessions because we find ourselves coveting even after certain desires are fulfilled.

What are certain things you're inclined to long for?

In what ways can we battle resentment toward God and the people who have the status or possessions we crave?

How can you identify coveting in others? How can you identify coveting in yourself?

Coveting Isolates and Robs Us

Coveting keeps us focused on our immediate circumstances and prevents us from looking ahead. But we need to make sure that we live our lives with the proper perspective—what we experience now is temporary and eternity awaits us. Jesus lived His life with this perspective. He didn't seek the riches this world has to offer but instead sought after our eternal salvation.

In Luke 12, as Jesus was talking to His disciples, someone from the surrounding crown broke through and changed the issue at hand.

> [13] Someone from the crowd said to Him, "Teacher, tell my brother to divide the inheritance with me."
> [14] "Friend," He said to him, "who appointed Me a judge or arbitrator over you?" [15] He then told them, "Watch out and be on guard against all greed because one's life is not in the abundance of his possessions."
> [16] Then He told them a parable: "A rich man's land was very productive. [17] He thought to himself, 'What should I do, since I don't have anywhere to store my crops? [18] I will do this,' he said. 'I'll tear down my barns and build bigger ones and store all my grain and my goods there. [19] Then I'll say to myself, "You have many goods stored up for many years. Take it easy; eat, drink, and enjoy yourself."'
> [20] "But God said to him, 'You fool! This very night your life is demanded of you. And the things you have prepared—whose will they be?'
> [21] "That's how it is with the one who stores up treasure for himself and is not rich toward God."
> When asked about an inheritance issue, Jesus responded in a friendly yet firm manner with a question: "Who appointed Me a judge or arbitrator over you?"
> LUKE 12:13-21

It's difficult to read this question overlooking the sarcasm, but there is truth present. Jesus will one day be the Judge of all; in this moment, however, He wasn't sent to deal with sibling bickering.

When has coveting caused a breakdown in your family? In your friendships?

Jesus continued, warning the man and the crowd about where this request stemmed from—greed, or covetousness. We must beware of coveting in every form that it may present itself to us because it takes our eyes off eternal things and sets them exclusively on earthly things.

To illustrate the danger of this limited perspective, Jesus went on to tell the crowd a parable in verses 16-20. A rich man's land had a productive season, a sign of financial blessing. Since his land yielded a good harvest, he decided to save the extra. His barns were capable of storing all that he needed, but he decided to tear them down and build bigger ones in order to keep everything he had just reaped. On top of this, it seems as if he had decided to retire. He was choosing to eat, drink, and enjoy himself because he had goods that would last him for years.

Many of us would applaud this man for his ingenious investment. However, this man was selfish. Look at the use of pronouns in his monologue. He was concerned only with himself. He didn't give thanks to God for the blessing, nor did he choose to be generous with others. Then enters God: "You fool! This very night your life is demanded of you. And the things you have prepared—whose will they be?" What a terrifying response! Not only did God negate the man's plan, but He also informed him that he would die that very evening. Everything he had just come into possession of—wealth, security, status—was now gone.

Jesus closed the parable with these haunting words: "That's how it is with the one who stores up treasure for himself and is not rich toward God." This statement should strike fear into all of our hearts. Would we be so greedy that we would choose not to be generous toward God?

What is the connection between greed and coveting? How does generosity toward others relate to being generous toward God?

We must understand that everything we would desire outside of Christ is temporary. The latest gadgets will become outdated. The latest fashion trends will be destroyed by age. Homes and buildings will crumble to the ground. Cars will succumb to rust. Only the treasure that we have in Christ will last forever. But we must also understand that the possessions we do have ultimately belongs to God. We shouldn't envy what others have been given, but choose to be faithful with what He has entrusted to us. In this way, we'll show Him that we can be trusted with more.

In what ways should an eternal perspective shape our plans in the present? How does coveting rob us of an eternal perspective?

How are the Tenth Commandment and First Commandment related?

3 The Gospel Gives Contentment

The Bible shows us that possessions and relationships don't satisfy. But we all still have an inward desire to search for satisfaction, and the road to satisfaction eventually leads us back to God. He is the eternal One. He'll never leave us or forsake us.

Paul learned this truth after he was called to ministry. He sought to follow the traditional laws of Judaism in order to pursue righteousness. He was so zealous for God that he even persecuted those who believed and taught the way of Jesus. Yet nothing Paul had pursued ever brought him forgiveness or satisfaction.

Paul met Jesus (see Acts 9) and came to understand that everything he had been seeking after was useless. Paul then believed that the sacrifice of Christ was enough to pay for his sin and the resurrection of Christ was true. He began following Jesus and preaching the gospel in different cities. He would plant churches as he traveled and would then write letters to the churches to encourage them. In chapter 4 of his Letter to the Philippians, Paul encouraged the believers in Philippi with the secret of being content in all circumstances:

> [10] I rejoiced in the Lord greatly that once again you renewed your care for me. You were, in fact, concerned about me but lacked the opportunity to show it. [11] I don't say this out of need, for I have learned to be content in whatever circumstances I am. [12] I know both how to have a little, and I know how to have a lot. In any and all circumstances I have learned the secret of being content—whether well fed or hungry, whether in abundance or in need. [13] I am able to do all things through Him who strengthens me. [14] Still, you did well by sharing with me in my hardship.
>
> **PHILIPPIANS 4:10-14**

Paul found his joy in the Lord continually, and he found yet another reason to rejoice in the fact that the church in Philippi cared for him. He was glad they provided for him in his moments of need. But Paul's heart wasn't dependent on his circumstances. He wouldn't allow his surroundings to steal his joy. Even as he wrote this letter in prison, he was still able to say that he could be content in whatever circumstance he would find himself. It's easy to say these words in times of wealth and prosperity but harder behind prison walls and in chains.

Remember, we've already seen that wealth and prosperity don't satisfy. Those wouldn't help Paul. In prison, he was separated from others, but he was able to find contentment in all circumstances because he'd never be separated from the love of Christ. Nothing else could satisfy his soul.

How would you define contentment? Is there such a thing as holy discontent?

In what circumstances might it be good to desire something more?

Philippians 4:13—"I am able to do all things through Him who strengthens me"—is often misused as a slogan in the realm of sports or achieving goals. Our focus on individual pursuits apart from the gospel can cause us to misinterpret this verse. It's true that Christ enables us to accomplish much for Him, but in this context Paul was describing his ability to be content whether in good or bad times. Because of what God had given him in Christ, he found the purest satisfaction that anyone could ever experience.

A heart gripped by the gospel finds its satisfaction in God and enjoys His gifts. We don't have to wonder about fulfilling our needs because God has already promised to take care of them. This is why Jesus could tell His disciples with confidence, "Therefore I tell you, don't worry about your life, what you will eat; or about the body, what you will wear. For life is more than food and the body more than clothing" (Luke 12:22-23).

Jesus assured His followers that their needs would be provided for because God would be the One to care for them. They didn't need to covet material possessions because God would give them everything they needed. They didn't have to desire after what the world offers because the greatest treasure is found in Christ. Eternal life, security, and hope are given to those who believe through the power of the gospel.

In what ways is the gospel the answer to coveting? What new desires does the gospel give us?

What are some ways you've heard Philippians 4:13 used out of its context of contentment? What other biblical principles might apply in these cases?

GROUP STUDY

Warm Up

William (Bill) Wallace served as a medical missionary in China for 15 years, through numerous political uprisings, World War II, and the Communist takeover of China. He gave of his time, talents, and even food to love the Chinese people he ministered to. It was said by the Chinese, "He was one of us. He accepted our portion—all of it." After the Communist takeover, Bill was falsely charged with espionage and subjected to inhumane treatment, brainwashing, and torture. He died a martyr's death on February 10, 1951. Wallace experienced poverty and loneliness, but remained content in his Lord even to the end.[2]

Read Philippians 4:10-11.

> [10] I rejoiced in the Lord greatly that once again you renewed your care for me. You were, in fact, concerned about me but lacked the opportunity to show it. [11] I don't say this out of need, for I have learned to be content in whatever circumstances I am.

Think about this statement: "He was one of us. He accepted our portion—all of it." What "portion" is God asking you to accept?

How does coveting hinder our mission?

How does being content and generous support our mission?

In what ways are you learning contentment in any circumstance?

We're not defined by our possessions. We know whether we're coveting or living with an eternal perspective by keeping track of our heart—our time, thoughts, emotions, and finances. Everything we do will show if we covet a grand lifestyle or if we're mindful toward the kingdom of God. As we desire God's kingdom, we'll see our blessings and possessions being used for the spreading of the gospel to those who need to turn from their covetousness and find contentment in the only One who can satisfy.

Discussion

Our covetous desires point to our ultimate need to have a relationship with God. We seek after wealth because we're spiritually poor. We seek after possessions, yet everything we have is a gift from His hand. All relationships with created beings point to our need for the all-fulfilling relationship with our Creator. Sin has corrupted our ability to see the truth, but the gospel sets us free to understand true contentment.

Use this time to share what God has revealed as you connect the dots and pursue the gospel. Some of the questions below are from your daily reading assignments. They will guide your small-group discussion.

1. What does coveting look like? In your own words, how would you define it? How concerned are you about the sin of coveting?

2. What are certain things you are inclined to long for? In what ways can we battle resentment toward God and the people who have the status or possessions we crave?

3. When has coveting caused a breakdown in your family? What about your friendships?

4. What is the connection between greed and coveting? How does generosity toward others relate to being generous toward God?

5. In what ways should an eternal perspective shape our plans in the present? How docs coveting rob us of an eternal perspective?

6. How is the Tenth Commandment ("Do not covet") related to the First Commandment ("No other gods")? What is the relationship between coveting and the sin of Adam and Eve in the garden of Eden?

7. In what ways is the gospel the answer to coveting? What new desires does the gospel give us?

Conclusion

As believers, trusting the Lord with our lives will lead us to be content in any and all circumstances. Through this contentment, we can be mindful of those who need love and care, and especially the gospel. Many wander into the church seeking community yet leave lonely. Some churches attempt to help people through various groups and activities. While these strategies may work for some, still others continue on their way, wondering if anyone cares. It's important that we keep an eye out for those who need care and show them the love of Jesus because we have been shown the love of Jesus and are content in it.

Spend some time praying this for you and for your group:

> "God, help me learn the secret to finding contentment in You.
> Free me from my own thoughts of living to please myself. Show
> me how to love and serve others and I love and serve You. In all
> things, Jesus, help me find satisfaction in You. Amen."

1. William J. Fallis, as quoted in *Holman Illustrated Bible Dictionary*, "Covet, Covetous," ed. Chad Brand, Charles Draper, and Archie England, (Nashville: Holman Bible Publishers, 2003), 360.
2. Daniel L. Akin, *10 Who Changed the World* (Nashville: B&H, 2012), 29-46.
3. Billy Graham, in *Billy Graham in Quotes*, ed. Franklin Graham (Nashville: Thomas Nelson, 2011), 161.

Everything that we see about us that we count as our possessions only comprises a loan from God, and it is when we lose sight of this all-pervading truth that we become greedy and covetous.[3]

BILLY GRAHAM

NOTES

SMALL-GROUP TIPS

Reading through this section and utilizing the suggested principles and practices will greatly enhance the group experience. First is to accept your limitations. You cannot transform a life. Your group must be devoted to the Bible, the Holy Spirit, and the power of Christian community. In doing so your group will have all the tools necessary to draw closer to God and to each other—and to experience heart transformation.

GENERAL TIPS:

- Prepare for each meeting by reviewing the material, praying for each group member, and asking the Holy Spirit to work through you as you point to Jesus each week.

- Make new attendees feel welcome.

- Think of ways to connect with group members away from group time. The amount of participation you have during your group meetings is directly related to the amount of time you connect with your group members away from the group meeting. Consider sending e-mails, texts, or social networking messages encouraging members in their personal devotion times prior to the session.

MATERIALS NEEDED:

- Bible

- Bible study book

- Pen/pencil

PROVIDE RESOURCES FOR GUESTS:

- An inexpensive way to make first-time guests feel welcome is to provide them a copy of your Bible study book. Estimate how many first-time guests you can expect during the course of your study, and secure that number of books. What about people who have not yet visited your group? You can encourage them to visit by providing a copy of the Bible study book.

SMALL-GROUP VALUES

Meeting together to study God's Word and experience life together is an exciting adventure. Here are values to consider for small-group experiences:

COMMUNITY: God is relational, so He created us to live in relationship with Him and one another. Authentic community involves sharing life together and connecting on many levels with others in our group.

INTERACTIVE BIBLE STUDY: God gave the Bible as our instruction manual for life. We need to deepen our understanding of God's Word. People learn and remember more as they wrestle with truth and learn from others. Bible discovery and group interaction will enhance spiritual growth.

EXPERIENTIAL GROWTH: Beyond solely reading, studying, and dissecting the Bible, being a disciple of Christ involves marrying knowledge and experience. We do this by taking questions to God, opening a dialogue with our hearts, and utilizing other ways to listen to God speak (other people, nature, circumstances, etc.). Experiential growth is always grounded in the Bible as God's primary revelation and our ultimate truth-source.

POWER OF GOD: Processes and strategies will be ineffective unless we invite and embrace the presence and power of God. In order to experience community and growth, Jesus needs to be the centerpiece of our group experiences, and the Holy Spirit must be at work.

REDEMPTIVE COMMUNITY: Healing best occurs within the context of community and relationships. It's vital to see ourselves through the eyes of others, share our stories, and ultimately find freedom from the secrets and lies that enslave our souls.

MISSION: God has invited us into a larger story with a great mission of setting captives free and healing the broken-hearted (see Isa. 61:1-2). However, we can only join in this mission to the degree that we've let Jesus bind up our wounds and set us free. Others will be attracted to an authentic, redemptive community.

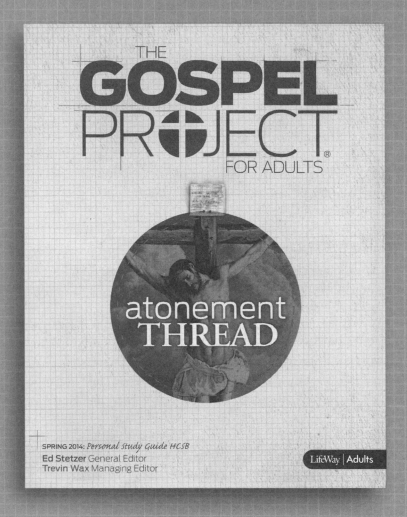

Continue the journey with The Gospel Project® ongoing studies...

Enjoying The Gospel Project?
If your group meets regularly, consider adopting
The Gospel Project as an ongoing Bible study series.

NEW STUDIES RELEASE EVERY THREE MONTHS.

Web: gospelproject.com
Twitter: @Gospel_Project
Facebook: TheGospelProject